EXPLORING THE STATES

New Hampshire

THE GRANITE STATE

by Emily Schnobrich

BLASTOFF!
5
READERS

BELLWETHER MEDIA • MINNEAPOLIS, MN

Note to Librarians, Teachers, and Parents:

Blastoff! Readers are carefully developed by literacy experts and combine standards-based content with developmentally appropriate text.

Level 1 provides the most support through repetition of high-frequency words, light text, predictable sentence patterns, and strong visual support.

Level 2 offers early readers a bit more challenge through varied simple sentences, increased text load, and less repetition of high-frequency words.

Level 3 advances early-fluent readers toward fluency through increased text and concept load, less reliance on visuals, longer sentences, and more literary language.

Level 4 builds reading stamina by providing more text per page, increased use of punctuation, greater variation in sentence patterns, and increasingly challenging vocabulary.

Level 5 encourages children to move from "learning to read" to "reading to learn" by providing even more text, varied writing styles, and less familiar topics.

Whichever book is right for your reader, Blastoff! Readers are the perfect books to build confidence and encourage a love of reading that will last a lifetime!

This edition first published in 2014 by Bellwether Media, Inc.

No part of this publication may be reproduced in whole or in part without written permission of the publisher. For information regarding permission, write to Bellwether Media, Inc., Attention: Permissions Department, 5357 Penn Avenue South, Minneapolis, MN 55419.

Library of Congress Cataloging-in-Publication Data

Schnobrich, Emily.
 New Hampshire / by Emily Schnobrich.
  pages cm. – (Blastoff! readers. Exploring the states)
 Includes bibliographical references and index.
 Summary: "Developed by literacy experts for students in grades three through seven, this book introduces young readers to the geography and culture of New Hampshire"– Provided by publisher.
 ISBN 978-1-62617-028-5 (hardcover : alk. paper)
 1. New Hampshire–Juvenile literature. I. Title.
 F34.3.S36 2014
 974.2–dc23
                                                                              2013004898

Printed in the United States of America, North Mankato, MN.

Table of
Contents

Where Is New Hampshire?

New Hampshire is a small, triangular state with towering mountains and sandy beaches. It is one of the six states that make up **New England**. This region forms the northeast corner of the United States.

New Hampshire shares its northern border with Canada. Maine is its neighbor to the east. To the south is Massachusetts. The Connecticut River separates New Hampshire from Vermont in the west. A small stretch of New Hampshire's southeast corner touches the Atlantic Ocean. The state capital, Concord, lies in the south.

New York

Canada

Maine

Did you know?
New Hampshire has a city called Sandwich. The town and the food were named after John Montagu, the Fourth Earl of Sandwich.

Connecticut River

Vermont

White Mountain
National Forest

Sandwich ●

New Hampshire

Concord ★

Portsmouth ●

Manchester ●

Atlantic Ocean

Nashua ●

Massachusetts

History

Before Europeans arrived, **Native** Americans such as the Pennacook people made their homes in New Hampshire. English traders came to settle the area in 1623. Eventually, the people of New Hampshire wanted independence from England. After the **Revolutionary War**, New Hampshire became one of the original thirteen states.

Revolutionary War

New Hampshire Timeline!

1603: Martin Pring is the first English explorer to visit New Hampshire.

1629: John Mason names New Hampshire after Hampshire, England.

1741: England makes New Hampshire a colony.

1776: New Hampshire is the first colony to declare independence from England.

1788: New Hampshire becomes the ninth U.S. state.

1808: Concord becomes the state capital.

1853: New Hampshire native Franklin Pierce becomes the fourteenth U.S. President.

1938: The Great New England Hurricane of 1938 destroys much of New Hampshire.

1986: New Hampshire teacher Christa McAuliffe is one of seven crewmembers aboard space shuttle *Challenger*. The shuttle explodes shortly after launching.

1996: Jeanne Shaheen is the first woman to be elected Governor of New Hampshire.

Franklin Pierce

The Great New England Hurricane damage

Christa McAuliffe

The Land

New Hampshire is a hilly, rocky state. The stunning White Mountains tower in the north. Tree-covered hills dot the land in the south. Many lakes and rivers cross New Hampshire. The largest lake, Lake Winnipesaukee, shimmers in the center of the state. In the southeast, lowlands end in coastal beaches.

Summers in New Hampshire are short and cool. Winters are long and snowy. The weather up in the mountains can be extremely cold and windy. Every day, the mountains and ocean affect the weather in unexpected ways.

fun fact

A unique rock formation on the side of Cannon Mountain looked like a human face. Sadly, the "Old Man of the Mountain" crumbled in 2003.

New Hampshire's Climate

average °F

spring
Low: 25°
High: 44°

summer
Low: 48°
High: 67°

fall
Low: 31°
High: 48°

winter
Low: 6°
High: 25°

The White Mountains

Did you know?
Mount Washington was hit by record wind speeds in 1934. Gusts reached 231 miles (372 kilometers) per hour!

The White Mountains form several different ranges. Peaks in the Presidential Range are named after famous U.S. Presidents. Mount Washington stands tall above all the others. At 6,288 feet (1,917 meters), it is New England's highest point.

White Mountain National Forest sits within the mountains. It spreads over many smaller peaks that dip below the **tree line**. Part of the Appalachian Trail runs through here. This famous footpath winds all the way from Maine to Georgia. Hikers can spend seven months trekking from end to end.

Mount Washington

fun fact

An average of 23 feet (7 meters) of snow piles up on Mount Washington each year. That is higher than a house!

Wildlife

Forests cover more than four-fifths of New Hampshire. Birch, pine, maple, and spruce trees grow everywhere. In fall, the leaves burst into color. They blanket New Hampshire's mountains in fiery **foliage**. Wild vines, shrubs, and berries are common underfoot. In summer, wildflowers such as goldenrod and wild aster speckle the countryside.

Deer, black bears, and moose stroll through New Hampshire's forests. Squirrels, foxes, and mink scurry nearby. Birds such as falcons, eagles, and ducks soar and waddle about. Trout and bass fill New Hampshire's sparkling lakes and rivers.

fox

falcon

goldenrod

mink

Cog Railway train

Flume Gorge

People from all over New England flock to the White Mountains. They enjoy breathtaking views as they ski, hike, and camp among the peaks. Three different railroads climb through the mountains. Visitors can travel to the top of Mount Washington on board the 145-year-old Cog Railway train.

covered bridge

More than 100 waterfalls flow throughout New Hampshire. Outdoor adventurers take trips to the Flume **Gorge**. They spend the day exploring this mossy granite valley and admiring the sparkling waterfalls within it. People driving through the countryside can rattle over covered bridges that are more than 100 years old.

Portsmouth

Portsmouth looks out over the Atlantic Ocean. The city's location once made it an important trading center. Now it is known for its historic buildings and a large **naval** shipyard that repairs submarines.

Portsmouth is a wonderful walking city with a lot of sidewalk cafés, shops, and parks. Several old houses now serve as museums. These grand old places paint a picture of wealthy society in early America. The Governor John Langdon House is a **colonial** mansion that features stunning wood carvings.

Governor John Langdon House

17

Working

Many of New Hampshire's workers design and produce computers and electronics. Others serve the state's **tourists** at hotels, ski resorts, and restaurants. They also work in theaters, give tours at history museums, and welcome visitors to state parks.

Out in the country, farmers grow apples, vegetables, and **ornamental** trees and plants. Miners dig for granite that is crushed into gravel for roads and gardens. Workers chop down trees that are processed into paper. Others tap trees to make New Hampshire's famous maple syrup.

Where People Work in New Hampshire

manufacturing
9%

farming and
natural resources
1%

government
11%

services
79%

Playing

New Hampshirites love to camp, ski, and hike in the mountains. Some take to the wilderness to hunt deer or ducks. Others rent boats for a day of fishing on the open sea. Both locals and tourists are drawn to the White Mountains when the fall leaves are prettiest.

The people of New Hampshire are proud of their history. Visiting historical buildings and museums is a common pastime. Dance, theater, and music events are also popular. In summer, the people of Portsmouth gather on picnic blankets in Prescott Park. They listen to live music under the stars.

New England Ski Museum

New Hampshire Stew

Ingredients:

- 1/8 pound of salt pork, cut into 1/4-inch cubes
- 2 tablespoons butter
- 1 pound stew meat (beef or game), cubed
- 3 carrots, sliced into 1-inch pieces
- 2 potatoes, cut into eighths
- 1 onion, sliced
- 1 garlic clove, crushed
- 1 bay leaf
- 1 1/2 cups beef broth
- 1 1/2 cups vegetable broth
- 1 tablespoon flour

Directions:

1. In a medium-sized pot, brown salt pork cubes in 1 tablespoon of butter until crisp. Drain on a paper towel.

2. Brown meat cubes in remaining fat. Add carrots, potatoes, onion, garlic, bay leaf, and broths.

3. Simmer covered for one hour, or until meat is tender.

4. Mix remaining butter with flour until smooth. Stir into stew. Cook 5 minutes longer to thicken. Remove bay leaf and serve immediately.

Did you know?
Apple cider is New Hampshire's state drink. Most orchards press their own cider and sell it in the fall.

pickled vegetables

The people of New Hampshire enjoy **hearty** foods. Hunters bring home deer, moose, and other **game** to be made into sausages or stews. There is also plenty of fresh seafood. Local restaurants serve sandwiches stuffed with bright pink lobster or fluffy white crab meat. Creamy clam **chowder** hits the spot on a cold winter's night.

Apples, pumpkins, berries, and maple syrup fill the stands at farmers' markets all over the state. Home **canning** is a popular way to preserve the fall and summer harvest. New Hampshire cooks make jams, sauces, and **pickled** vegetables to store all year round.

24

**Pittsfield
Hot Air Balloon Rally**

New Hampshire is full of festivals that celebrate nature and farming. The town of Keene puts on its famous Pumpkin Festival every October. Pumpkin carving is the main event. At night, thousands of glowing jack-o-lanterns line Keene's main street.

The Hillsborough and Pittsfield hot air balloon festivals are two spectacular summer events. Brightly colored hot air balloons take off into the sky. Visitors can pay to take a ride or watch from the ground. When it gets dark, balloon pilots turn up the flames to create a glowing sea of color.

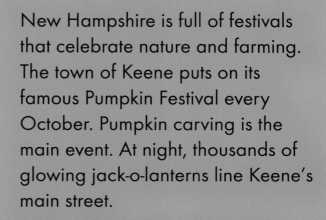

fun fact

Keene was the first town to win the Guinness World Record for "most jack-o-lanterns ever assembled in one place at one time."

Strawbery Banke isn't just a delicious-sounding name. It is a large outdoor museum in Portsmouth. It shows what life was like when the city was a **seaport** community long ago. The museum includes 42 **restored** buildings from as early as 1695.

knitting

coopering

Actors in costumes make the experience more realistic. They invite visitors to take part in historic activities such as weaving, knitting, and **coopering**. The Victorian Children's Garden includes a two-story tree house and a butterfly garden. A stroll through Strawbery Banke is a stroll through time. It brings New Hampshire's natural beauty and colonial history to life.

Fast Facts About New Hampshire

New Hampshire's Flag

New Hampshire's flag is blue. The state seal is in the center. It features a ship and a sunrise. Golden leaves and nine stars circle the seal. The stars show that New Hampshire was the ninth state.

State Flower
purple lilac

State Nickname:	The Granite State
State Motto:	"Live Free or Die"
Year of Statehood:	1788
Capital City:	Concord
Other Major Cities:	Manchester, Nashua
Population:	1,316,470 (2010)
Area:	9,280 square miles (24,035 square kilometers); New Hampshire is the 46th largest state.
Major Industries:	manufacturing, services, lumber
Natural Resources:	lumber, sand, gravel, granite
State Government:	400 representatives; 24 senators
Federal Government:	2 representatives; 2 senators
Electoral Votes:	4

State Bird
purple finch

State Animal
white-tailed deer

Glossary

canning—a method of preserving fruits and vegetables by cooking them and storing them in airtight jars

chowder—a thick, creamy soup made with seafood or vegetables

colonial—relating to the American colonies settled by the British in the 1600s and 1700s

coopering—the making of barrels, buckets, and other containers out of narrow lengths of wood

foliage—the leaves of plants

game—wild animals hunted for food or sport

gorge—a deep, narrow valley with steep, rocky sides

hearty—filling and satisfying

native—originally from a specific place

naval—relating to a navy or its ships

New England—a group of six states that make up the northeastern corner of the United States

ornamental—for decoration

pickled—preserved in an acidic liquid

restored—repaired or returned to the original condition

Revolutionary War—the war between 1775 and 1783 in which the United States fought for independence from Great Britain

seaport—a sea harbor where ships can dock

tourists—people who travel to visit another place

tree line—the highest point where trees can grow on a mountain

To Learn More

AT THE LIBRARY

Ciarleglio, Lauren. *New Hampshire: Past and Present*. New York, N.Y.: Rosen Central, 2011.

Cunningham, Kevin. *The New Hampshire Colony*. New York, N.Y.: Children's Press, 2012.

Miller Shannon, Terry. *New Hampshire*. New York, N.Y.: Children's Press, 2009.

ON THE WEB

Learning more about New Hampshire is as easy as 1, 2, 3.

1. Go to www.factsurfer.com.

2. Enter "New Hampshire" into the search box.

3. Click the "Surf" button and you will see a list of related Web sites.

With factsurfer.com, finding more information is just a click away.

Index

The images in this book are reproduced through the courtesy of: Ron and Patty Thomas Photography/ Getty Images, front cover (bottom); North Wind Picture Archives/ Alamy, p. 6; (Collection)/ Prints & Photographs Division/ Library of Congress, p. 7 (left); Everett Collection Inc/ Alamy, p. 7 (middle); Science and Society/ SuperStock, p. 7 (right); NobleImages/ Alamy, p. 8 (small); DeniseBush, pp. 8-9; DenisTangneyJr, pp. 10-11, 11 (small); Menno Schaefer, p. 12 (top); Glenn Price, p. 12 (middle); Chris Hill, p. 12 (bottom); Arndt Sven-Erik/ Age Fotostock, pp. 12-13; James A. Harris, p. 14 (top); Pchoui, p. 14 (bottom); Brian Jannsen/ Age Fotostock/ SuperStock, pp. 14-15; Andre Jenny/ Alamy, p. 16 (top); Ian Dagnall/ Alamy, p. 16 (bottom); Mira/ Alamy, pp. 16-17; AP Photo/ Charles Krupa/ Associated Press, p. 18; Gerenme, p. 19; Jared Alden/ Aurora Open/ SuperStock, p. 20 (top); David R. Frazier Photolibrary, Inc./ Alamy, p. 20 (bottom); Jay Boucher, pp. 20-21; MSPhotographic, p. 22; Pilipphoto, p. 23 (top); Monticello, p. 23 (bottom); Juliaf, pp. 24-25; Rod Chronister, p. 25; Andre Jenny Stock Collection Worldwide/ Newscom, pp. 26-27; Washington Imaging/ Alamy, p. 27 (top); John Elk III/ Alamy, p. 27 (bottom); Pakmor, p. 28 (top); Melica, p. 28 (bottom); Steve Byland, p. 29 (left); Tom Reichner, p. 29 (right).